Going Swimming

By Diane Church

Photographs by Chris Fairclough

W

FRANKLIN WATTS

RNID
THE ROYAL NATIONAL
INSTITUTE FOR DEAF PEOPLE

Rowan and Annice are cousins.
They are also good friends. Rowan is deaf.
This weekend Annice is coming to stay
with Rowan and his mum.

Rowan is taking Annice
swimming and then they
are going to the Deaf Club.

Rowan was born deaf. He hardly hears anything but he sometimes wears a hearing aid to help him hear.

2

Rowan decides to watch a video while he waits for Annice to arrive. "Can I watch this one?" Rowan asks his mum. Rowan's mum is deaf too. They use sign language to talk to each other.

Sign language includes handshapes, movement and facial expression.

At last, Annice arrives and Rowan gets to the door first. "It's great to see you again!" says Annice. "You too!" Rowan replies.

Rowan knows that there is someone at the door because the lights in the house flash off and on when the doorbell is pressed.

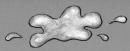

They catch up on their news.
"We're going swimming next,"
Rowan tells Annice and her mum.
"That sounds fun," says Annice's
mum.

Rowan and his
mum lipread.
It's not easy;
many sounds, such
as "p" and "m"
look similar when
you say them.

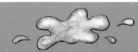

While they are eating, the lights flash again because the telephone is ringing.
"It's Dad," Rowan's mum reads.
"He'll see us later at the Club."
"O.K." Rowan says.

Rowan's mum uses a textphone. This has a small screen and a keyboard attached to it. The caller's words appear on the screen. Rowan's mum types in her answer and it is read by the person using a textphone at the other end.

It's time to set off for the pool.
Rowan is excited. "I can swim
a long way now," he tells Annice's mum.

At the pool, Rowan's mum signs to the assistant and pays for the tickets. "See you in the water," says Annice.

The assistant faces Rowan's mum and speaks clearly. This helps Rowan's mum to lipread.

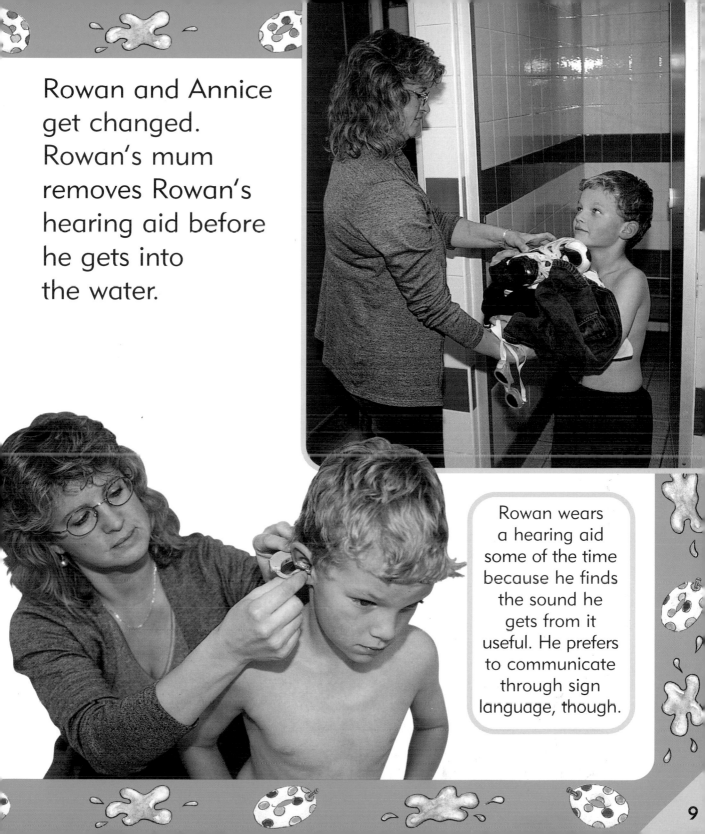

Rowan and Annice get changed. Rowan's mum removes Rowan's hearing aid before he gets into the water.

Rowan wears a hearing aid some of the time because he finds the sound he gets from it useful. He prefers to communicate through sign language, though.

Together the two friends step into the water.
"It's freezing!" Annice squeals.
"You'll soon get used to it," her mum
tells her.

They have fun
splashing about.
"One, two, three..."
counts Rowan as
they jump into
the pool.

Next they decide
to go down the
slide. "This is
brilliant!" Rowan
thinks to himself.

As they play, a girl swims behind Rowan.
He steps back and bumps into her.
"Watch out!" she says crossly.

Annice explains that Rowan is deaf and didn't hear the girl coming up behind him. "Sorry!" the girl says as she swims off.

A person who is deaf may not hear if you come up behind them. You need to look at them directly to communicate.

Soon Rowan's mum beckons him to the side of the pool.

"Time for you two to get out if you want a pizza before we go the Deaf Club," she tells him.

Rowan's mum gets his attention by doing something he can see. One good way of getting a deaf person's attention is by waving at them.

At the restaurant, the two friends
decide what to have.
"I'm starving!" says Rowan.

While they eat, Rowan tells Annice all about the Deaf Club by signing at her. "Annice, you can practise your sign language there," her mum suggests.

If hearing people learn a little bit of sign language, deaf people find it easier to communicate with them.

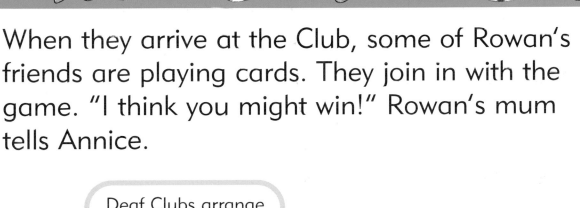

When they arrive at the Club, some of Rowan's friends are playing cards. They join in with the game. "I think you might win!" Rowan's mum tells Annice.

Deaf Clubs arrange games and sport activities. They are great places for deaf and hearing people to get together.

After the card game, Rowan plays pool with his dad. Rowan's dad is deaf too. It's soon time for Rowan and Annice to leave. "Time to go!" Annice says.

The best way of attracting a deaf person's attention if they are not looking at you is by gently tapping them on the shoulder.

Rowan doesn't want to go. He pretends he doesn't understand what Annice is saying. "I can't hear you!" he jokes.

Annice pushes Rowan towards the door. "It's been a really great day!" she laughs.

Being deaf means finding different ways to communicate. It doesn't stop you having fun!

Facts about deaf people

★ Deaf people look like hearing people. Unless they are wearing a hearing aid or using sign language, it isn't possible to tell that they are deaf.

★ Deaf people communicate in different ways depending on how much they can hear. They may speak, lipread, use sign language or a combination of all three.

★ Sign language is a complete language that deaf people use to express themselves fully. It's not a mimed version of a spoken language.

★ Different sign languages are used in Britain, the United States and Australia even though the people all speak English. This is because sign languages are different from spoken languages.

★ Most deaf children are born deaf or become so at an early age. Only one deaf child in 10 has a deaf mum or dad.

Here are some signs you can share with your friends:

◄This sign means "hello" and "good".

This sign means "goodbye". ▶

◄ This sign means "thank you".

This sign means "come here". ▶

Try to be helpful

1. Try learning sign language. It's fun to use a different language!

2. When you speak to a deaf person, don't shout. If they are wearing a hearing aid, shouting can cause great distress. Shouting also makes it harder for a deaf person to work out what you're saying.

3. If the person is lipreading, look at them and don't eat or drink while you speak.

4. If you are not making yourself understood, say it again using different words.

5. Remember, deaf people are like hearing people, they just can't hear!

Further information and addresses

Royal National Institute for Deaf People (RNID)
19-23 Featherstone Street
London EC1Y 8SL
Email: information@rnid.org.uk
www.rnid.org.uk

National Deaf Children's Society (NDCS)
15 Dufferin Street
London EC1Y 8UR

National Centre for Language and Literacy
Bulmershe Court,
Earley
Reading RG6 1HY
E-mail: ncll@reading.ac.uk

Australian Association of the Deaf
Suite 513, 149 Castlereagh Street
Sydney, NSW 2000
Australia
www.aad.org.au
Email: aad@aad.org.au

Index

This edition 2003

Franklin Watts
96 Leonard Street
London
EC2A 4XD

Franklin Watts Australia
45-51 Huntley Street
Alexandria
NSW 2015

© 2000 Franklin Watts

ISBN: 0 7496 5187 3

Dewey Decimal Classification
Number: 362.4

A CIP catalogue record for
this book is available from the
British Library.

Printed in Malaysia

Consultants: Philippa Smart and Anne
Hodgson (RNID); Beverley Matthias (REACH)
Editor: Samantha Armstrong
Designer: Louise Snowdon
Photographer: Chris Fairclough
Illustrator: Eliz Hüseyin

With thanks to: Lisa and Rowan Warnock and their family,
Annice Weatherly-Sinclair and her family, Nottingham Deaf
Society, Rushcliff Leisure Centre and Pizza Hut, Nottingham.